All Night Near The Water

Jim Arnosky

G. P. Putnam's Sons
New York

For Jennifer, Danielle, Erin, Willie,
Elizabeth, and Meghan.

G. P. Putnam's Sons, a division of
The Putnam & Grosset Group,
200 Madison Avenue, New York, NY 10016.
G. P. Putnam's Sons, Reg. U.S. Pat. & Tm. Off.
Published simultaneously in Canada.
Printed in Hong Kong by South China Printing Co. (1988) Ltd.
Book designed by Patrick Collins. Text is set in Kennerley.

Library of Congress Cataloging-in-Publication Data
Arnosky, Jim.   All night near the water / Jim Arnosky.   p.   cm.
1. Mallard—Juvenile literature.   [1. Mallard. 2. Ducks.] I. Title.
QL696.A52A76 1994   598.4′1—dc20   93-31078   CIP   AC
ISBN 0-399-22629-X

10 9 8 7 6 5 4 3 2 1   First Impression

In the golden glow of a summer evening, mother mallard leads her ducklings

away from the nest in the
tall meadow grass...

to the lake.

The ducklings follow in a row
around the shoreline weeds,

through a driftwood maze,

to a sandbar where they will
spend their first night
near the water.

Mother mallard tries to sleep
but her ducklings are not sleepy.

They listen to the frogs,

and spy on a heron catching fish.

The ducklings watch the dark shapes of bats flying in the twilight.

At nightfall the ducklings see
lights twinkling over the water.

A hungry pike cruises by.
Mother mallard calls softly for
her ducklings to huddle near.

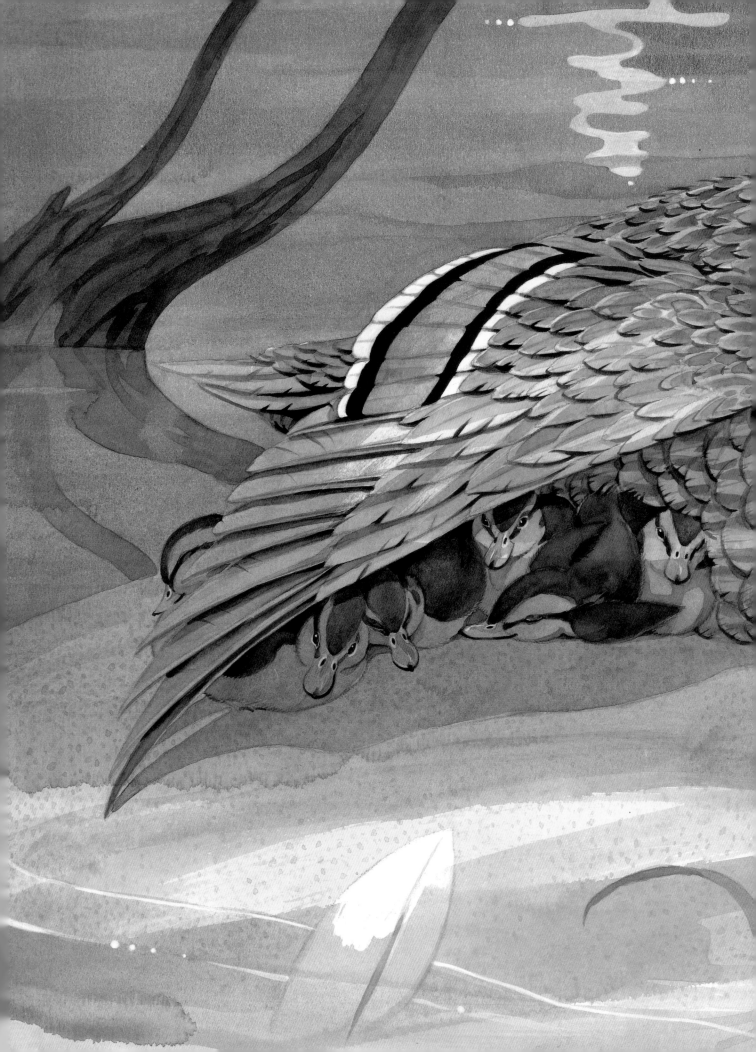

She covers them with her wings
and presses them against her sides.

Through the darkest hours of the night, mother mallard keeps her ducklings hidden, safe, and warm.

As the sun slowly rises,
a sudden breeze ripples the lake.

When the world is light again,
mother mallard flaps her wings

and quacks out loud. Wake up!
It's time to take a morning swim.

A new day has begun.